Hot Math Topics

Problem Solving, Communication, and Reasoning

Time and Money

TICKETS

ADULTS.. $4.00
KIDS... $3.00
BIRDS.. $2.00

grade 2

Carole Greenes
Linda Schulman Dacey
Rika Spungin

Dale Seymour Publications®
Parsippany, New Jersey

This book is published by

Dale Seymour Publications
An imprint of Pearson Learning
299 Jefferson Road, P.O. Box 480
Parsippany, New Jersey 07054-4080

www.pearsonlearning.com
1-800-321-3106

Managing Editor: Catherine Anderson
Senior Editor: John Nelson
Project Editor: Mali Apple
Production/Manufacturing Director: Janet Yearian
Sr. Production/Manufacturing Coordinator: Fiona Santoianni
Design Director: Phyllis Aycock
Cover and Interior Illustrations: Jared Lee
Text and Cover Design: Tracey Munz
Composition and Computer Graphics: Alan Noyes

ISBN 0-7690-0004-5

3 4 5 6 7 8 9 10-ML- 06 05

This Book Is Printed
On Recycled Paper

Contents

Introduction

Why Was *Hot Math Topics* Developed?

The *Hot Math Topics* series was developed for several reasons:

- to offer children practice and maintenance of previously learned skills and concepts
- to enhance problem solving and mathematical reasoning abilities
- to build literacy skills
- to nurture collaborative learning behaviors

Practicing and maintaining concepts and skills

Although textbooks and core curriculum materials do treat the topics explored in this series, their treatment is often limited by the lesson format and the page size. As a consequence, there are often not enough opportunities for children to practice newly acquired concepts and skills related to the topics, or to connect the topics to other content areas. *Hot Math Topics* provides the necessary practice and mathematical connections.

Similarly, core instructional programs often do not do a very good job of helping children maintain their skills. Although textbooks do include reviews of previously learned material, they are often limited to sidebars or boxed-off areas on one or two pages in each chapter, with four or five exercises in each box. Each set of problems is intended only as a sampling of previously taught topics, rather than as a complete review. In the selection and placement of the review exercises, little or no attention

is given to levels of complexity of the problems. By contrast, *Hot Math Topics* targets specific topics and gives children more experience with concepts and skills related to them. The problems are sequenced by difficulty, allowing children to hone their skills. And, because they are not tied to specific lessons, the problems can be used at any time.

Enhancing problem solving and mathematical reasoning abilities

Hot Math Topics present children with situations in which they may use a variety of problem solving strategies, including

- designing and conducting experiments to generate or collect data
- guessing, checking, and revising guesses
- organizing data in lists or tables in order to identify patterns and relationships
- choosing appropriate computational algorithms and deciding on a sequence of computations
- using inverse operations in "work backward" solution paths

For their solutions, children are also required to bring to bear various methods of reasoning, including

- deductive reasoning
- inductive reasoning
- proportional reasoning

For example, to solve clue-type problems, children must reason deductively and make inferences about mathematical relationships in order to generate candidates for the solutions and to home in on those that meet all of the problem's conditions.

To identify and continue a pattern and then write a rule for finding the next term or block in that pattern, children must reason inductively.

To make trades and compute unit prices, children must reason proportionally.

To estimate or compare magnitudes of numbers, or to determine the type of number appropriate for a given situation, children must apply their number sense skills.

Building communication and literacy skills

Hot Math Topics offers children opportunities to write and talk about mathematical ideas. For many problems, children must describe their solution paths, justify their solutions, give their opinions, or write or tell stories.

Some problems have multiple solution methods. With these problems, children may have to compare their methods with those of their peers and talk about how their approaches are alike and different.

Other problems have multiple solutions, requiring children to confer to be sure they have found all possible answers.

Nurturing collaborative learning behaviors

Several of the problems can be solved by children working together. Some are designed specifically as partner problems. By working collaboratively, children can develop expertise in posing questions that call for clarification or verification, brainstorming solution strategies, and following another person's line of reasoning.

What Is in *Time and Money*?

This book contains 100 problems and tasks, 40 involving time and 60 involving money. The mathematics content, the mathematical connections, the problem solving strategies, and the communication skills that are emphasized are described below.

Mathematics content

Time problems and tasks require children to

- tell time to the nearest minute
- order events temporally
- estimate and compute elapsed time in minutes, days, or weeks
- match events to amounts of time
- interpret and create schedules
- use calendars to identify days and dates

Money problems and tasks require children to

- identify values of sets of coins
- compare values of sets of coins
- construct different sets of coins with the same value
- compute with amounts of money less than one dollar and with whole-dollar amounts
- use the dollar sign and the decimal point or the cents sign to write amounts of money

Mathematical connections

In these problems and tasks, connections are made to these other topic areas:

- graphs
- algebra
- statistics

Problem solving strategies

Time and Money problems and tasks offer children opportunities to use one or more of several problem solving strategies.

- **Formulate Questions:** When data are presented in displays or text form, children must pose one or more questions that can be answered using the given data.

- **Complete Stories:** When confronted with an incomplete story, children must supply the missing information and then check that the story makes sense.

- **Organize Information:** To ensure that all possible solution candidates for a problem are considered, children may have to organize information using a picture, list, diagram, or table.

- **Guess, Check, and Revise:** In some problems, children have to identify candidates for the solution and then check whether those candidates match the conditions of the problem. If the conditions are not satisfied, other possible solutions must be generated and verified.

- **Identify and Continue Patterns:** To identify the next term or terms in a sequence, children have to recognize the relationship between successive terms and then generalize that relationship.

- **Use Logic:** Children have to reason deductively, from given clues, to make inferences about the solution to a problem. They must also reason proportionately to determine which of two buys is better.

Communication skills

Problems and tasks in *Time and Money* are designed to stimulate communication.

As part of the solution process, children may have to

- describe their thinking steps
- describe patterns
- find alternate solution methods and solution paths
- identify other possible answers
- write problems for classmates to solve
- compare solutions and methods with classmates

These communication skills are enhanced when children interact with one another and with the teacher. By communicating both orally and in writing, children develop their understanding and use of the language of mathematics.

How Can *Hot Math Topics* Be Used?

The problems may be used as practice of newly learned concepts and skills, as maintenance of previously learned ideas, and as enrichment experiences for early finishers or more advanced students.

They may be used in class or assigned for homework. If used during class, they may be selected to complement lessons dealing with a specific topic or assigned every week as a means of keeping skills alive and well. Because the problems often require the application of various problem solving strategies and reasoning methods, they may also form the basis of whole-class lessons whose goals are to develop expertise with specific problem solving strategies or methods.

The problems may be used by children working in pairs or on their own. Within each topic—*time* and *money*—the problems are sequenced from least to most difficult. The selection of problems may be made by the teacher or the children based on their needs or interests. If the plan is for children to choose problems, you may wish to copy individual problems onto card stock and laminate them, and establish a problem card file.

To facilitate record keeping, a Management Chart is provided on page 6. The chart can be duplicated so that there is one for each child. As a problem is completed, the space corresponding to that problem's number may be shaded. An Award Certificate is included on page 6 as well.

How Can Children's Performance Be Assessed?

Time and Money problems and tasks give you opportunities to assess children's

- knowledge of time and money
- problem solving abilities
- mathematical reasoning methods
- communication skills

Observations

Keeping anecdotal records helps you to remember important information you gain as you observe children at work. To make observations more manageable, limit each observation to a group of from four to six children or to one of the areas noted above. You may find that using index cards facilitates the recording process.

Discussions

Many of the *Time and Money* problems and tasks allow for multiple answers or may be solved in a variety of ways. This built-in richness motivates children to discuss their work with one another. Small groups or class discussions are appropriate. As children share their approaches to the problems, you will gain additional insights into their content knowledge, mathematical reasoning, and communication abilities.

Scoring responses

You may wish to holistically score children's responses to the problems and tasks. The simple scoring rubric below uses three levels: high, medium, and low.

Portfolios

Having children store their responses to the problems in *Hot Math Topics* portfolios allows them to see improvement in their work over time. You may want to have them choose examples of their best responses for inclusion in their permanent portfolios, accompanied by explanations as to why each was chosen.

Children and the assessment process

Involving children in the assessment process is central to the development of their abilities to reflect on their own work, to understand the assessment standards to

High	Medium	Low
• Solution demonstrates that the child knows the concepts and skills.	• Solution demonstrates that the child has some knowledge of the concepts and skills.	• Solution shows that the child has little or no grasp of the concepts and skills.
• Solution is complete and thorough.	• Solution is complete.	• Solution is incomplete or contains major errors.
• The child communicates effectively.	• The child communicates somewhat clearly.	• The child does not communicate effectively.

which they are held accountable, and to take ownership for their own learning. Young children may find the reflective process difficult, but with your coaching, they can develop such skills.

Discussion may be needed to help children better understand your standards for performance. Ask children such questions as, "What does it mean to communicate *clearly*?" "What is a *complete* response?" Some children may want to use the high-medium-low rubric to score their responses. Others may prefer to use a simple visual evaluation, such as these characters:

Participation in peer-assessment tasks will also help children to better understand the performance standards. In pairs or small groups, children can review each other's responses and offer feedback. Opportunities to revise work may then be given.

What Additional Materials Are Needed?

Although manipulative materials and measurement devices are not required for solving the problems, if they are available in the classroom, they may be useful for some children. For example, a clock face or real analog and digital clocks, minute timers, tiles of various shapes, play money (coins and bills), and calendars may be useful. For drawing purposes, colored pencils, crayons, and rulers should be readily accessible. Calculators are not required for any of the problems, although some children may find them beneficial.

When a problem or task is completed, shade the box with that number.

1	2	3	4	5	6	7	8	9	10
11	12	13	14	15	16	17	18	19	20
21	22	23	24	25	26	27	28	29	30
31	32	33	34	35	36	37	38	39	40
41	42	43	44	45	46	47	48	49	50
51	52	53	54	55	56	57	58	59	60
61	62	63	64	65	66	67	68	69	70
71	72	73	74	75	76	77	78	79	80
81	82	83	84	85	86	87	88	89	90
91	92	93	94	95	96	97	98	99	100

Award Certificate

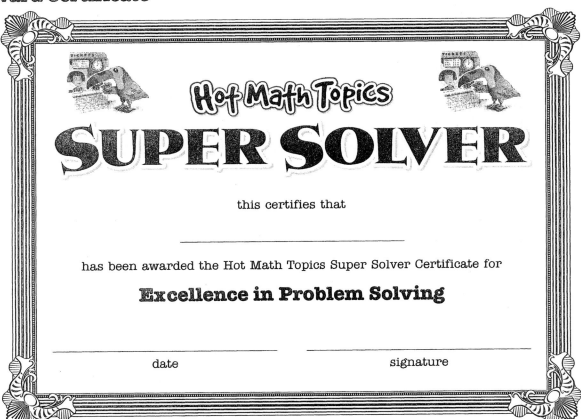

Hot Math Topics

SUPER SOLVER

this certifies that

_____

has been awarded the Hot Math Topics Super Solver Certificate for

Excellence in Problem Solving

_____   _____
date   signature

©Addison Wesley Longman, Inc./Published by Dale Seymour Publications®

Problems
and Tasks

Put the pictures in order.
Write 1, 2, 3, 4.

Brushing teeth	**Walking into school**	**Going to bed**	**Reading in school**
_____	_____	_____	_____

- -

Compare.
Which takes more time?

Jump 10 times.   Write your name
10 times.

How did you decide?

Nigel and Diane are friends.

Nigel gets up at 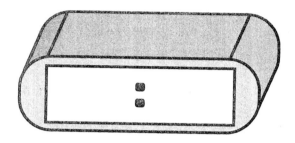 .

Diane gets up I hour earlier.

Show the time Diane gets up.

- -

Ask I0 children what time they wake up.

Make a table of their answers.

Times

What time do most of the children wake up?

Play Time

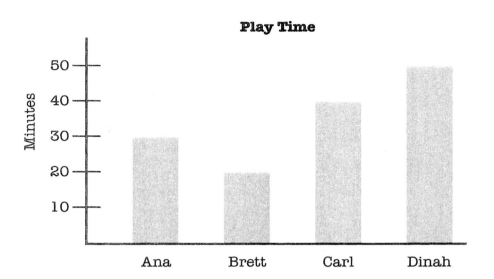

Make up a math problem about this graph. Solve your problem.

- -

Draw the hands.

I hour before 3:00

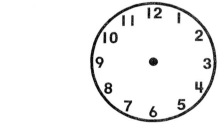

2 hours after 4:00

5 hours before 12:00   12 hours before 8:00

©Addison Wesley Longman, Inc./Published by Dale Seymour Publications®

Think of special times in your classroom.

Show a special time on each clock.

Tell what happens at that time.

Erika gets up at ⟨ 7:00 ⟩ **.**

She goes to school 2 hours later.

She has lunch 3 hours after she goes to school.

Show the time Erika has lunch.

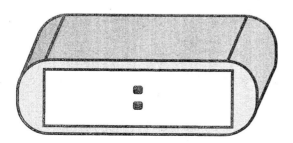

How is 8:00 in the morning different from 8:00 at night?

Write three ways they are different.

- -

Put the pictures in order to tell a story.

Write 1, 2, 3, 4.

_____

_____

_____

_____

You put a cake in the oven.

It bakes for 40 minutes.

Show the time when the cake is done.

- -

Keep track of your day.

Write something you do during each hour.

9:00 _____

10:00 _____

11:00 _____

12:00 _____

1:00 _____

2:00 _____

3:00 _____

Write 1, 2, 3, and 4 under the clocks.

1. Bryana left school at 3 o'clock.

2. One hour later she went out to play.

3. Two hours after playing she ate dinner.

4. She went to bed at 8:30.

_____   _____   _____   _____

- -

I played for 1 hour at the playground.

How many minutes did I play in the sandbox?

Fill in the blanks.

I woke up at _____ today.

My favorite time today is _____
because _____
_____.

I will go to sleep at about _____
tonight.

Today I will be awake for about
_____ hours.

The clock shows the time.

**How many more minutes until the
movie starts?**

Write all the dates for Tuesdays.

Look at those dates.

Tell about the patterns you see.

S	M	T	W	T	F	S
	1	2	3	4	5	6
7	8	9	10	11	12	13
14	15	16	17	18	19	20
21	22	23	24	25	26	27
28	29	30				

April

- -

What is the date?

- It is after October 7.
- It is before October 12.
- It is not a day that starts with a T.
- It is not Friday.

The date is October ____.

The day is _____.

October

S	M	T	W	T	F	S
		1	2	3	4	5
6	7	8	9	10	11	12
13	14	15	16	17	18	19
20	21	22	23	24	25	26
27	28	29	30	31		

Draw lines.

Match each clock to a clue.

Facts

- 30 minutes after 6:30
- 15 minutes before 8:00
- 30 minutes before 7:15
- 60 minutes after 6:15

Take turns. Work with a friend.

One person counts for 15 seconds:
"1 dinosaur, 2 dinosaur, . . . , 15 dinosaur."

The second person does the task until the counter finishes.

| | Number of Times ||
Task	name _____	name _____
Clap hands		
Write "math"		
Hop on one foot		

Record how many times the second person does the task.

Draw a picture.

Show what you do in the morning.

Write a story.

Tell what you do in the morning.

- -

Lucia's art class begins at 9:30.

How much longer will she have to wait?

Tell how you know.

Pick a month.

Tell about the special days in the month.

FEBRUARY July

November

Use the numbers on the sign.

Put a number in each blank.

The story must make sense.

The race started at _____ .

Meg finished the race at _____ .

She ran for _____ minutes.

Kiran took 10 minutes longer.

He finished at _____ .

The Halls went on a 2-week vacation.

They left on June 2.

When did they return?

It is the third Sunday.

How many days are there until the fourth Friday?

Tell how you know.

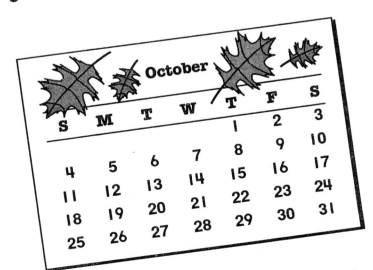

A   B   C

Which clock shows the time Jo's lesson starts? _____

Clues

- All the clocks show times in the morning.
- The lesson starts **after** 9 o'clock.
- The lesson is over **before** noon.
- The lesson is 1 hour long.

- -

9 hours

5 months   2 months   1 hour

Which time is closest to

- the time you sleep at night? _____
- the time you read each day? _____
- the time between the Fourth of July and Thanksgiving? _____

Make up three more questions about these times.

Trade questions with a friend.

We can say:

- "It is two fifteen."
- "It is a quarter past 2."
- "It is 15 minutes after 2."

Write two ways to tell each of these times:

_____   _____

_____   _____

It takes
1 second
to snap
my
fingers.

Finish these sentences.

It takes 1 minute to _____.

It takes 1 hour to _____.

It takes 1 day to _____.

It takes 1 year to _____.

Today is Wednesday, June 12.

Mari's library book is due in 10 days.

On what day of the week is the book due?

Tell how you know.

My birthday is Friday, April 4.

Today is 2 days before my birthday.

What day is it?

What is the date?

Bus Schedule		
Bus	Leaves	Arrives
1	7:30	8:00
2	6:45	7:45
3	7:45	8:00
4	7:00	7:40
5	7:50	8:00

**Cal's bus took 10 minutes.
Which bus did Cal take?** _____

**Tanya's bus took 15 minutes.
Which bus did Tanya take?** _____

**Write a "Which bus?" question.
Answer your question.**

- -

**Rubin says it takes him 1 minute
to count to 60.**

- Make a list of things that
  take you 1 minute to do.

**Julia says it takes her
1 hour to make cookies.**

- Make a list of things that
  take you 1 hour to do.

**Compare your lists with a
friend's lists.**

Fill in the times in the schedule.

Facts

- The bus stops at Kalona at 12:00.

- The bus stops at Kane 4 hours after it stops at Kalona.

- The bus stops at Marion 1 hour before it stops at Kalona.

Bus Schedule		
Stop	City	Time
1	Marion	
2	Kalona	
3	Milton	
4	Hillview	
5	Kane	

- The bus stops at Hillview 30 minutes before it stops at Kane.

- The bus stops at Milton 2 hours before it stops at Hillview.

The movie is 2 hours and 10 minutes long.

The movie ends at 4:30.

What time does the movie start?

37

Write a story about bikes.

Use these times in your story.

- -

Which program is 30 minutes longer than the news program?

38

TV Schedule

Time	Program
8:00	movie
9:30	holiday special
10:15	sports
10:30	weather
10:45	news
11:00	mystery
12:00	talk show

You put the turkey into the oven at 3:00.

You will take the turkey out at _____ .

- -

Activity	10:00–10:30	10:30–11:00	11:00–11:30
Basketball	×	×	×
Biking	×	×	
Canoeing		×	×
Swimming	×		×
T-ball	×	×	

Camp Schedule

The ×'s are the lessons.

How many more minutes of basketball lessons are there than swimming lessons?

Tell how you know.

Circle the sets of coins that have the same value.

- -

I have 16¢.

I have 4 coins.

What coins do I have?

= 1¢ 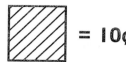 = 5¢   = 10¢

How much is the pattern of stickers worth?

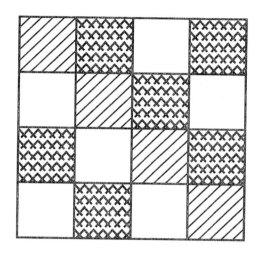

- -

Lani bought these three stickers.

She spent 12¢.

How much did the rainbow sticker cost?

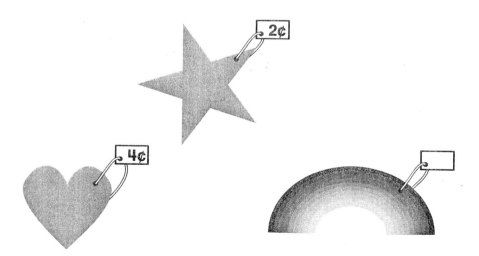

Fill in the shapes with numbers.

The story must make sense.

Carlos has ☐ nickels.

He has ◯ dimes.

He has △ ¢ in all.

How much will the family pay for their tickets?

You can buy these stickers:

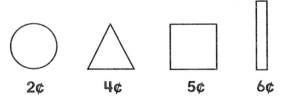

2¢   4¢   5¢   6¢

Which sticker animal costs more, A or B?

How much more?

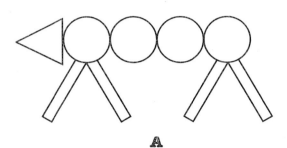

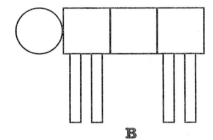

A   B

- -

Hani and Jan shared the coins equally.

How much money did each get?

**Jamie has
these coins:**

**Lelia has
these coins:**

**Lelia and Jamie want to have the same
amount of money.**

What coins should Lelia give to Jamie?

- -

Draw lines.

Match each price to a fruit.

Facts

- The pear costs the most.

- The orange costs more than the banana.

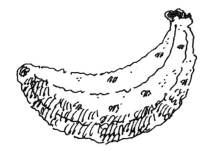

 40¢

 29¢

 55¢

Draw lines. Match each person to the coins.

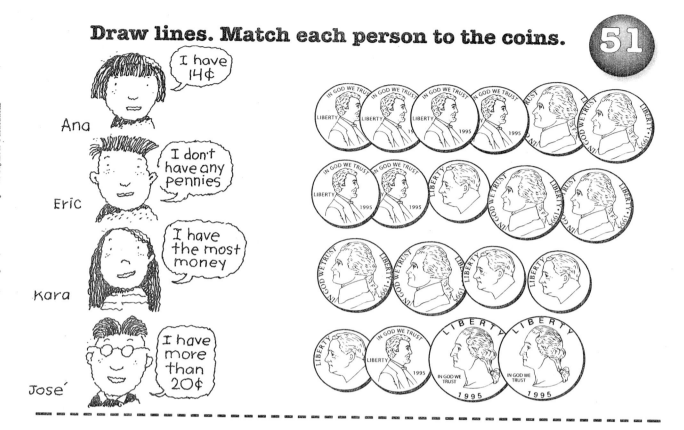

Ana — I have 14¢

Eric — I don't have any pennies

Kara — I have the most money

José — I have more than 20¢

Talk with a friend.

Make a list of things that cost less than one dollar.

I have

How much more money do I need to buy the piggy bank?

Tell how you know.

- -

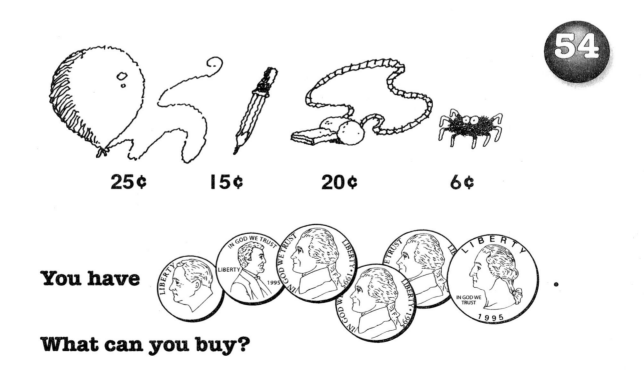

25¢   15¢   20¢   6¢

You have

What can you buy?

Sarah's money: **Alec's money:**

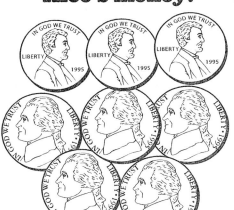

Who has more money?

How can you tell?

You will need: a paper bag, a penny, a nickel, a dime, and a quarter.

Work with a friend. Take turns.

One person puts 3 coins in the bag. The other does not look!

The other person feels the coins in the bag and guesses the amount of money.

How much money does Rika have?

Show the same amount of money using a different set of coins.

Name the coins.

Show this amount of money with the fewest coins.

Name the coins.

- -

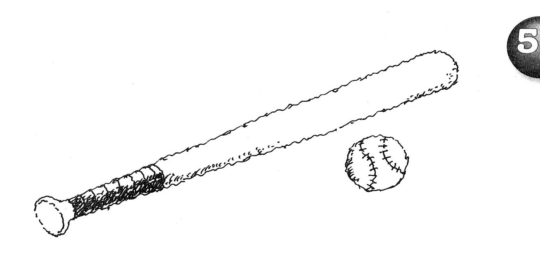

Write numbers so that the story makes sense.

Kai bought a ball for $ _____ .

He bought a bat for $ _____ .

The bat costs $ _____ more than the ball.

Kai spent $ _____ in all.

Find the correct amount on the sign.

Clues

- It is less than 3 dimes.
- It is more than 3 nickels.
- It is not 16¢.

The amount is _____ .

Who has more money?
Give two ways to tell.

David's money:

Jeni's money:

Masako has the most money.

Kim has more money than Luis.

Find each amount. Then write the name of the person.

Amount _____   **Amount** _____   **Amount** _____

Name _____   **Name** _____   **Name** _____

- -

You have  .

Which of these can you make? Tell how.

6¢ _____

12¢ _____

16¢ _____

20¢ _____

25¢ _____

30¢ _____

31¢ _____

41¢ _____

Choose 2 of these coins.

- How much money is it?

Choose 2 other coins.

- How much money is it?

How many different amounts of money can you make?

Compare your answer with a friend's answer.

- -

What do the toys cost?

Facts

Prices

$3 $6 $4

- The car costs less than the train.
- Together the train and the car cost $9.

The car costs _____.

The boat costs _____.

The train costs _____.

Sandra said, "I had

and I bought a pen for 40¢."

Kyle said, "I had

and I bought a yo-yo for 50¢."

Who has more money left?

How can you tell? Give two ways.

- -

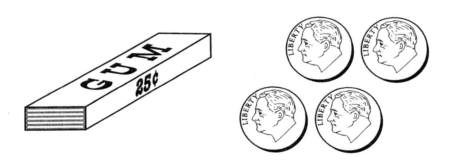

Write a story problem to fit the picture.

Give the answer to your problem.

Draw a sticker doll that costs more than this doll.

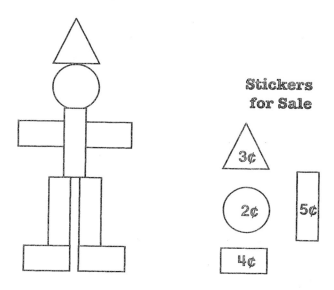

Stickers
for Sale

3¢

2¢

5¢

4¢

How much does your doll cost?

- -

Alex has this money:

Taylor has twice as much money as Alex.

How much money does Taylor have?

Lana started with these coins:

She bought apple juice.

How much change did she get?

40¢

- -

What are the coins in the bag?

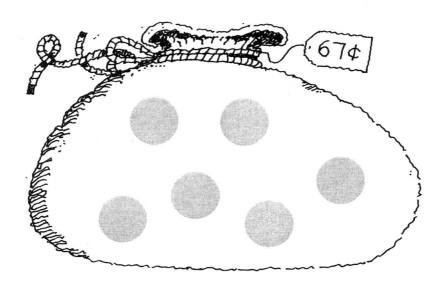

67¢

Work with a friend.

How many different ways can you have
20¢ in coins?

Make a list. Show the ways.

Ways to Make 20¢

Dimes	Nickels	Pennies

Tell how Danya and Ben can share
the money.

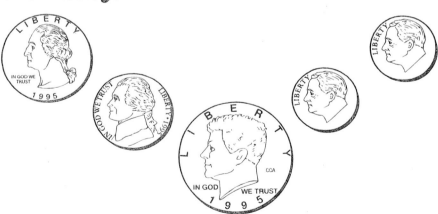

How much money will each person get?

You have more than

You have less than

You do not have 23¢.

How much money do you have?

Ali had these coins:

She bought a sports mug.

She got 35¢ back.

How much did the mug cost?

How much money is in the dolphin bank?

Clues

- There are 10 coins.
- 5 of the coins are pennies.
- 3 of the coins are dimes.
- The rest of the coins are nickels.

I have these coins:

How much more money do I need to buy the duck bank?

99¢

How much money does Juan have?

Facts

- He doesn't have any pennies.
- He has less than 75¢.
- He has more than 40¢.

Draw coins Juan could have.

40¢

85¢

31¢

65¢

- -

You have these coins:

You want to have a dollar.

What other coins do you need?

Choose two amounts of money.

Write a money problem.

The answer must be on the sign.

10¢   5¢

15¢   25¢

Jimmy has 6 coins worth $1.

Jimmy has one half dollar.

What coins does Jimmy have?

Now find a different answer.

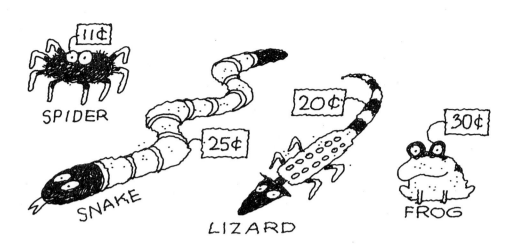

SPIDER 11¢

SNAKE 25¢

LIZARD 20¢

FROG 30¢

I spent 66¢.

I bought 3 toys.

What did I buy?

- -

You had 43¢.

You earned 2 dimes, 3 nickels, and 1 penny.

How much money do you have now?

Jess has 1 dollar and 2 quarters.

Ron has 4 quarters and 6 dimes.

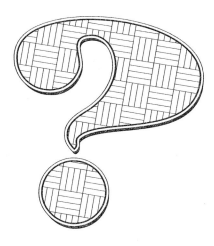

Who has more money?

Tell how you know.

- -

How much money could I have?

Clues

• I have more than 70¢.

• I have less than 94¢.

• I do not have any pennies.

Give all the answers.

Hani made a tally mark for every coin he has.

How much money does Hani have?

Hani's Money

Coin	Number
half dollar	|
quarter	||
dime	|||
nickel	|
penny	||||

There are 9 coins in the pattern.

What is the total amount of money?

Use the numbers shown.

Use each number once.

Make sure the story makes sense.

Marla has $ _____ .

She buys a CD for $ _____ .

She buys a tape for $ _____ .

The tape costs $5 less than the CD.

Now Marla has $ _____ left.

6 25 12 7

Jeff had $5.00.

Maria had no money.

Jeff gave Maria this money:

Now who has more money, Jeff or Maria?

How do you know?

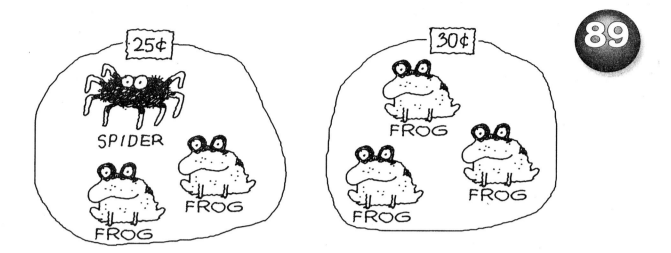

How much does a toy spider cost?

How did you decide?

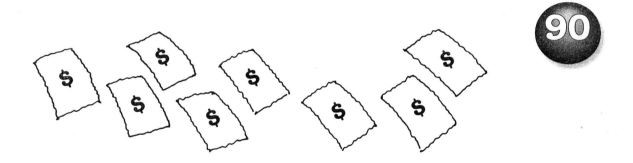

I have 8 bills.

I have one five-dollar bill.

The rest are one-dollar bills.

How much money do I have?

Work with a friend.

Meela had

She bought some stamps.

Now she has

What stamps did Meela buy?

Make a list.

92

You want to make a bead chain.

You have 30¢ to spend on beads.

 10¢ each   5¢ each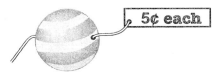

How many different groups of beads could you buy?

For each group, tell the number of each type of bead.

Carl has one dollar in coins.

What coins does Carl have?

Facts

- He has 2 quarters.
- He has more dimes than nickels.

He has _____ quarters.

He has _____ dimes.

He has _____ nickels.

He has no pennies.

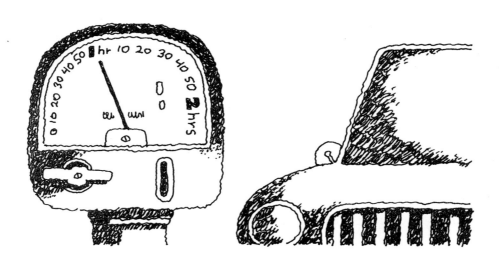

It costs 5¢ for 10 minutes.

How much will it cost to park for 1 hour?

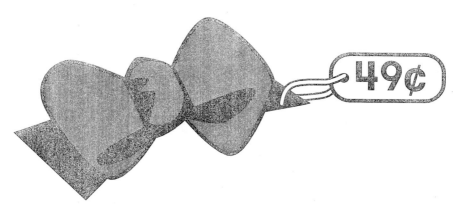

You work in a store.

Lili buys a bow.

She gives you $1.

Tell how you make the change.

How much is the change?

- -

Work with a friend.

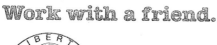

Choose two coins.

Choose two things.

Write a math problem about what
you chose.

Solve the problem.

Jin Lee has this money:

Alan has 25¢ more than Jin Lee.

Terry has 50¢ less than Alan.

Who has the most money?

How much does he have?

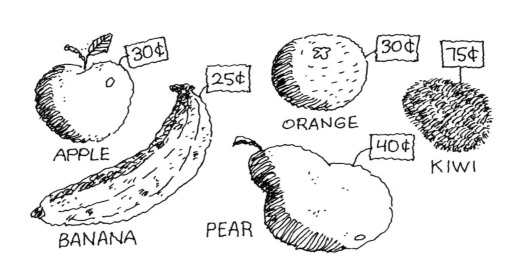

APPLE 30¢
BANANA 25¢
ORANGE 30¢
KIWI 75¢
PEAR 40¢

Spend $1.00. Make a fruit basket.

Tell the fruits you would use.

Can you use different fruits?

Find the missing price.
Tell how you found it.

20¢   40¢   ?¢

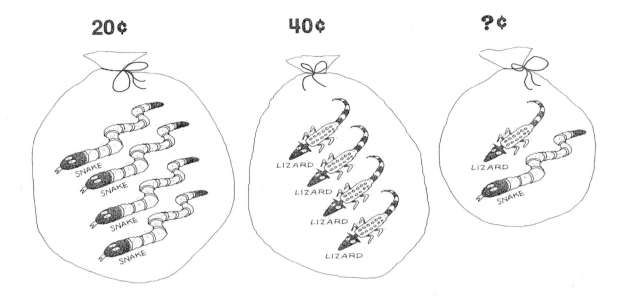

- -

Which is the better buy?
Tell how you know.

 # Answers

1. Answers will vary

2. Answers will vary. Generally, writing takes more time than jumping. Students might experiment to make the comparison.

3. 6:30

4. Answers will vary.

5. Answers will vary.

6. From left to right the clocks should show 2:00, 6:00, 7:00, and 8:00.

7. Answers will vary.

8. 12:00

9. Answers will vary. Some possibilities:
   - It is light in the morning and dark at night.
   - I wake up at 8:00 in the morning. I go to sleep at 8:00 at night.
   - At 8:00 in the morning, people go to work. At 8:00 at night, they are home from work.
   - There are different programs on radio and television at 8:00 at night than at 8:00 in the morning.

10. 3, 2, 4, 1 or 2, 1, 3, 4 (left to right)

11. The clock should show 3:45.

12. Answers will vary.

13. 2, 4, 1, 3

14. 20 minutes

15. Answers will vary.

16. 90 minutes

17. The dates are 2, 9, 16, 23, and 30. Some patterns children might notice:

- Each date is 7 more than the previous date.
- The difference between every other date is 14.
- The numbers are in the order even, odd, even, odd, even.

18. October 9; Wednesday

19. The order of the times is 7:00, 7:45, 6:45, 7:15.

20. Answers will vary.

21. Answers will vary.

22. 45 minutes; Explanations will vary.

23. Answers will vary.

24. 12:30, 1:00, 30, 1:10

25. June 16 (Children may say June 15 if they count exactly 14 days.)

26. 5 days; Explanations will vary.

27. clock B

28. 9 hours, 1 hour, 5 months; Questions will vary.

29. Possible answers: "30 minutes after 4," "four thirty," "half past 4"; "nine thirty-five," "35 minutes after 9," "25 minutes before 10"

30. Answers will vary.

31. Saturday; Explanations will vary.

32. Wednesday, April 2

33. bus 5; bus 3; Questions will vary.

34. Answers will vary.

35. 11:00, 12:00, 1:30, 3:30, 4:00

36. 2:20

37. Answers will vary.

38. holiday special

39. 5:00

40. 30 minutes; One possible solution method: There are 3 basketball lessons lasting 30 minutes each. There are 2 swimming lessons lasting 30 minutes each. This is one more basketball lesson than swimming lesson.

41. Students should circle the nickel-penny-quarter set and the penny-2 nickels-2 dimes set.

42. 3 nickels and 1 penny

43. 76¢

44. 6¢

45. Answers will vary.

46. $16

47. B costs 5¢ more (41¢ versus 36¢).

48. 23¢

49. 1 penny and 1 nickel

50. banana 29¢, orange 40¢, pear 55¢

51. Ana has 4 pennies and 2 nickels; Eric has 2 nickels and 2 dimes; Kara has 1 penny, 1 dime, and 2 quarters; and José has 2 pennies, 2 nickels, and 1 dime.

52. Answers will vary.

53. 7¢; Explanations will vary.

54. Answers will vary. The total must be 51¢ or less.

55. Sarah has 36¢ and Alec has 28¢, so Sarah has more money. Possible explanation:

   • Figure out how much each person has, and compare the totals.

   • Trade Sarah's 3 dimes for 6 nickels. Then Sarah has 7 nickels and 1 penny while Alec has 5 nickels and 3 pennies. Since Sarah has more nickels, she has more money.

57. 51¢; Collections will vary.

The fewest coins are two, 1 half dollar and 1 penny.

58. Answers will vary.

59. 27¢

60. David; Possible explanations:

   • Find the value of each set and compare them. David has 10¢ more than Jeni.

   • Trade Jeni's 8 nickels for 4 dimes. Then David has 1 more dime than Jeni.

61. Luis, 17¢; Masako, 30¢; Kim, 26¢

62. 6¢ (penny and nickel); 16¢ (penny, nickel, and dime); 25¢ (quarter); 30¢ (nickel and quarter); 31¢ (penny, nickel, and quarter); 41¢ (penny, nickel, dime, and quarter)

63. There are 6 possibilities: 2¢, 6¢, 10¢, 11¢, 15¢, and 20¢.

64. $3, $4, and $6

65. Sandra; Possible explanations:

   • Kyle spent 10¢ more than Sandra did, so he has 10¢ less left over.

   • Sandra had 68¢ and spent 40¢. She has 28¢ left. Kyle had 68¢ and spent 50¢. He has 18¢ left. Sandra has more money left.

66. Story problems will vary.

67. Drawings will vary, but dolls should cost more than 36¢.

68. $7.00

69. 5¢

70. 2 pennies, 1 nickel, 1 dime, and 2 quarters *or* 2 pennies, 3 nickels, and 1 half dollar

71. 9 ways (dimes-nickels-pennies): 2-0-0, 1-2-0, 1-1-5, 1-0-10, 0-4-0, 0-3-5, 0-2-10, 0-1-15, 0-0-20

72. One person gets the half dollar; the other gets the quarter, 2 dimes, and the nickel. Each person gets 50¢.

73. 24¢

74. 65¢

75. 45¢

76. 62¢

77. 65¢; Coin collections will vary.

78. You need 14¢. Possible answers: 14 pennies *or* 4 pennies and 2 nickels *or* 4 pennies and 1 dime *or* 9 pennies and 1 nickel

79. Problems will vary.

80. 3 nickels, 1 dime, 1 quarter, and 1 half dollar *or* 5 dimes and 1 half dollar

81. the spider (11¢), the snake (25¢), and the frog (30¢)

82. 79¢

83. Ron; Possible explanation: 4 quarters is 1 dollar, and 6 dimes is more than 2 quarters.

84. 75¢, 80¢, 85¢, or 90¢

85. $1.39

86. 48¢ (The repeating pattern is penny-nickel-dime.)

87. $25, $12, $7, $6

88. Jeff has more money. Possible explanation: Jeff gave Maria $2.45, so he has $2.55.

89. 5¢; Possible explanation: Three frogs cost 30¢ so one frog is 10¢. Two frogs and one spider is 20¢ plus 5¢.

90. $12

91. Meela spent 16¢, so she can buy any of these combinations (birds-kites-apples): 8-0-0, 5-2-0, 4-1-1, 3-0-2, 2-4-0, 1-3-1, 0-2-2

92. There are four groups: 6 beads for 5¢ *or* 4 beads for 5¢ and 1 bead for 10¢ *or* 2 beads for 5¢ and 2 beads for 10¢ *or* 3 beads for 10¢

93. 2 quarters, 4 dimes, 2 nickels *or* 2 quarters, 5 dimes, 0 nickels

94. 30¢

95. Possible answer: Count up from 49¢: 49¢ + 1¢ = 50¢. 50¢ + 50¢ = $1.00. The change is 1¢ + 50¢ = 51¢.

96. Problems will vary.

97. Jin Lee has $1.55. Alan has $1.80. Terry has $1.30. Alan has the most money.

98. Possible answers:
    - 1 apple, 1 orange, 1 pear
    - 2 apples, 1 pear
    - 2 oranges, 1 pear
    - 1 banana, 1 kiwi
    - 4 bananas

99. 15¢; A lizard costs 10¢. A snake costs 5¢. So a lizard and a snake cost 15¢.

100. 200 stickers for 99¢ is the better buy. Possible explanation: If 200 stickers are 99¢, then 100 stickers would be about 50¢—which is 50 more stickers than the other deal.